Praise from Amazon

The
Leadership
Secrets of
Squirrels

Other books by the author:

A Grave Misunderstanding
Flicker
Skeleton

The Leadership Secrets of Squirrels

More than 60 acorns of wisdom to make you a better leader—today!

Simon Silverback

Foreword by Robert L. Lorber
Co-author: *Putting the One Minute Manager to Work* and *One Page Management*

Translated from the original leaftext by
Len Boswell

To all I love
Without condition
To all I love
Without omission

Never doubt

Squirrels for nuts contend, and, wrong or right, for the world's empire kings ambitious fight. What odds? To us 'tis all the self-same thing: a nut, a world, a squirrel, and a king.

—Charles Churchill

Here Skugg
Lies snug
As a bug
In a rug

—Benjamin Franklin

The trunk sways
The root's deep
Safe are we
In our leafy keep

—Old Skugg

Contents

Part Three: 20 Secrets from the Nutground, 21

Foreword

At first glance, you may think this book is not to be taken seriously, something you will look at briefly and put away without much second thought. A book written by a squirrel? You've got to be kidding. Leadership is an important, serious subject in all aspects of our lives: business, government, education, sports, religion, and family.

Everyone has his or her own perspective on leadership, after all, so why should the perspective of a squirrel be less important? If there is even one acorn of wisdom here, even one idea makes us better.

I've been blessed to able to work with business leaders from all over the world. I've worked closely with hundreds of CEOs of corporations, senior business leaders at all levels, university leaders, a few country leaders, and community leaders, and most of them will love the fun concepts in this little book.

I know you are skeptical; there are thousands of books on leadership, and now one from a squirrel's perspective? I was skeptical too at first. The manuscript was shoved under my door, no more than a loosely bound pile of leaves, with markings as curious and unintelligible as hieroglyphs, looking more like the work of a sudden gust of wind than the work of a leader and fellow mammal. But once translated, the book grew on me, as I hope it does on you. I love creative new ways at looking at how we can help become better leaders in all aspects of our lives.

You may not agree with everything you read, but I can guarantee that you will have fun, learn, and never think of leadership, or squirrels, in quite the same way again.

For me and most of the people I work with in my consulting practice, leadership is about serving others. I'm not just talking about CEO's, presidents, and directors. I'm talking about anyone who is in a role that influences other people. Leadership is about making the world a better place for all of us, and my hope is that as you read some of the concepts in this book, you will be a better leader in all aspects of your life.

Please enjoy this practical, quick read, and hey, it's the best leadership book ever written by a squirrel.

—ROBERT L. LORBER

Preface

You have seen us in the trees, scampering (as you would put it) from branch to limb, seemingly without purpose, one of nature's furry wind-up toys. You have seen us chasing each other around tree trunks, like idiots (you would say). You have seen us frantically trying, and often failing, at the simple act of crossing a road. And you have seen us bury nuts and acorns everywhere, with little or no hope of ever finding them all again. You think us at best dull of brain and at worst a pest to be driven away or killed. We are the clowns on the lawn, the menace at the bird feeder, the kill on the road.

So why should you look to us for advice on leadership? I will spare you the long story, the one our parents used to tell us, ad nauseam, as the winter winds howled outside and we huddled with the others in our nest at the top of the great oak. The short of it is simply this: we are born to leadership, and you are not. What you humans know of leadership would barely fill an acorn cap, and you seem to jump from one theory to the next as deftly and as blithely as we leap from limb to branch. But where we have purpose you have only direction. So your first lesson is this:

Leadership without purpose is like a compass in the hands of a fool: any direction will do.

But I get ahead of myself. If you have picked up this book—or better yet, purchased it—you are probably a person who likes a little whimsy, or a little book, or both. Good, because the first thing a leader must be able to do is chitter—I mean *laugh*. And the second is to get to the point—quickly.

So let's get on with it.

—SIMON SILVERBACK

Introduction

This little book focuses on leadership secrets that we squirrels use every day, and you humans so often ignore. As Part I so clearly points out, however, this is not a book about leadership *theories*, so beyond this brief introduction you will find nary a mention nor a footnote on Burns, Jago, Fiedler, Jenkins, Hegel, Weber, Carlyle, Smith, Machiavelli, Stogdil, Confucius, or Plato. Neither will you find mentions of path-goal, contingency, situational, or charismatic-leader theory and the like. No again if you expect mentions of recent books on leadership. I haven't read them. I'm a squirrel for skugg's sake. Most would crush me with their weight. And frankly, they don't taste all that good, either.

No, what you will read here is based on my experience and on the teachings of Lindar the Elder, known affectionately and reverentially as "Old Skugg." Throughout, I have drawn quotes from his seminal work, *The Obsylarium*, which regrettably is largely out of leaf and unavailable these days. *Skugg* (also *skug* or *scug*), by the way, is 18th Century vernacular for *squirrel*.

Old Skugg led the Squirrel Rebellion of 1791 during the reign of Sciurus VII, invading the corn-rich fields of Belpre, Ohio, with an army of thousands low on acorns and high on appetite. After decimating its fields, he did the unfathomable (or as he would say later, "quite fathomable") by having his army *swim* across the Ohio

River to West Virginia and its waiting crops. Your General Sherman is said to have used some of Old Skugg's techniques in his march to the sea during your Civil War.

Old Skugg had his theories, too, but you will not find them here. Some do not translate well to your world, e.g., the critical importance of deliberative acorn-spinning in the decision-making process. Others, while appropriate, are just theories. No, what you will find here is his and my leadership secrets, tools you can use, or not use, when and as you wish.

Leadership is like the weather. We know what it is when we see it, but fail miserably in trying to create it. And though we think we can track it, measure it, and make reasonable predictions about its results, it remains one of the great mysteries—at least in theory.

Now . . .

Look into my eyes and follow the swishing of my tail. You are getting sleepy, sleepy, and you are now hypnotized. After reading this book, every time you see a squirrel, you will think of the lessons you have learned here and how you can apply them where you work. And you will pay a little homage to us by thinking, "Thank you, Old Skugg, for the teachings you have given us." If you are in a car, you will brake for us, giving us that little extra second or two so we can remember our own lessons. There. You will awaken now, at the count of three, feeling refreshed and eager to read this book from cover to cover. One, two, THREE . . .

Finally, you are probably wondering, *why a book on leadership written by a squirrel?* The only answer I can offer is, why not? Another, better question to ask is, why are you reading a book written by a squirrel? I think you would say, "Well, because leadership interests me," or, "Because I want to be a leader," or "Well, it looked like a great gift for my boss."

All three answers are good, especially the last. Only think beyond your boss. This book is a great gift for everyone you know, young and old, so buy more and buy often—even squirrels have to make a living.

Part One

Leadership Theory

"Theories come and theories go, but the latter is always preferable."

—Old Skugg

Yes, leadership is a theory. Bury yours here, as I would a nut—you can always come back and dig it up (I think). Now turn to Part Two.

Part Two

14 Secrets on Crossing a Road

"In the deadly swirl of battle, I have often ordered retreats and attacks simultaneously—and was right to do so."

—Old Skugg

Humans. You are so curious-strange. You wonder at an age-old question, *why did the chicken cross the road*, when you have probably never seen a chicken do that. And yet, you never seem to wonder why, in the face of all the danger, mayhem, and death, a squirrel crosses the road.

Never have you dreamed that a squirrel, by the simple act of crossing a road, could offer up no fewer than fourteen leadership lessons, or secrets. Some of these will make sense to you, others not. Some will seem to contradict others. That is as it should be. *Leaders must embrace contradictions every day.*

3

1

Know *why* you are crossing the road

"It's about the nuts, stupid!"

—Old Skugg

Every new venture requires a goal. "I will go to the other side of the road" is not a goal, it is an act, a direction. If that is the only thought you take with you, you are in for a world of hurt. You have no idea what you're going to do when you get there, and you place no relative value, or importance, on the crossing. The road is filled with danger. *Always know why you risk those dangers.*

For squirrels, it's usually about one thing. As Old Skugg used to say, "It's about the nuts, stupid!" * What is your goal? Whatever it is, you can capture it in Old Skugg's saying. Just fill in the blank:

It's about the _____, stupid!

---

*My editor tells me a variation on this phrase gained wide parlance among humans during and after a 20th Century political campaign. The human political strategist who first used it, James Carville, knows a nut when he sees one.

2

Know *when* to cross the road

"We crossed the river at dawn, when we were light of stomach, hungry for food, and believed in our hearts that we could swim."

—Old Skugg

I've lost a lot of friends and colleagues, leaders all, with good and noble goals, because they chose to cross roads when the conditions were not right. They'd each planned as if the roads were dry and the traffic light—to their great peril. So the question you must ask is, Is now the right time to act? Can you reach your goal now? Later? Ever? Look at the road carefully. *Leadership is often a matter of timing.*

3

Stick to your niche

"A leader out of his element is a leader likely to fail."

—Old Skugg

Squirrels almost always cross the road to gather more nuts, or to return home. If you have a singular purpose in crossing the road, and it's to do what you normally do, or complements what you normally do, so much the better. If you are crossing to do something different, something you have never done before, because you've seen others doing it and, hey, it seems like a good idea, beware. You must not only consider the road to be crossed, but the mysteries and obstacles that lie on the other side. Many a squirrel has crossed the road to find, well, whatever, never to return. Others tried to get back, realizing their mistake, only to find the road blocked, or impassable. Others tried to cross back and died in classic fashion, road kill for a day and a fine meal for crows and turkey vultures. Some few returned, only to find their nests destroyed and the nutground claimed by competitors. *So, if your goal in crossing is to do something new and un-squirrely, think long and hard, and don't.*

4

Lead, follow, or get squashed on the road

"We threw them into complete disarray, not by tactics, but by the singular terror of our headlong charge."

—Old Skugg

A popular road-kill theory is that squirrels skitter, feint, and juke back and forth in front of your car because they can't comprehend anything moving at them in a straight line, at great speed, that the situation is totally alien to them. Pish! I know what a car, a truck, or a kid on a bike can do to me! But the secret in avoiding them and crossing the road is: be decisive! *When you are faced with danger, make one decision, stick to it, and move as quickly as possible in one direction.* You may be going in the wrong direction, but at least you'll be making good time.

5

Indecision is a decision with consequences

"Not knowing which way to move an army is far worse than deciding not to move it at all."

—Old Skugg

To some of you, I'm sure, a squirrel darting to and fro is the epitome of indecision. But no, we are not like deer frozen in your headlights. What you perceive as indecision is actually a series of rapid decisions, and save for one—the last decision—half are right and half are wrong. (See Secret 6.)

However, even though squirrels are not by nature indecisive, your observation does present a valuable leadership lesson: *Indecision can have terrible consequences*. To be indecisive is to be frozen in the headlights, unsure of what to do next, and not willing or able to act. Four options are always available to you, but only the last three are acts of leadership.

INDECISION
NO DECISION
BAD DECISION
GOOD DECISION

Indecision is by far the worst. It is the waster of time and opportunity and advantage. No Decision, the close

9

bosom friend of Indecision, wastes time, but not necessarily at the expense of opportunity or advantage. Bad decisions happen; embrace them, learn from them, and remember that success is often the result of a long series of progressively lesser failures. Good decisions are treasures, but don't spend time admiring them. You have other decisions to make.

6

Too many quick decisions are worse than no decision

"The orders came in such rapid succession, and were so contrary, that all was chaos, the troops wondering more about what would come next than what they were then doing."

—Old Skugg

Some people take Leadership Secret 4 too much to heart. They think quick decisions are inherently good, so they often opt for a series of bad decisions, hoping that speed and luck will eventually point them in the right direction. Such people are far too fond of the phrase "midcourse correction." Alas, here is a lesson that too many squirrels can teach—the ultimate road-kill lesson.

7

Doubt is as keen a sword as confidence

"Doubt can destroy an army—or save it. Always be bold, even when doubt clamps your heart like the talons of a hawk."

—Old Skugg

When you see us in the road, you see confidence and doubt simultaneously. Where we are bold, we are also cautious. If doubt arises, we act on that doubt, probing it until we are satisfied, and then move on. Doubt is not a conservative approach, but a necessary approach, to action. When you proceed, proceed boldly, letting doubt keep you alert and at the ready without slowing you down. Although leaders may be conservative in their beliefs, they should not be conservative in their actions. *True leadership is the ability to act boldly in the presence of doubt.*

8

Old strategies often do not work for new situations

"If an enemy arrays its forces in a novel way, you must change your battle plan accordingly, or be prepared for a bloody outcome."

—Old Skugg

Sometimes experts stumble upon a truth while misinterpreting data. As I mentioned in Secret 4, squirrels do not die on the road because they are incapable of dealing with a new situation. But I will have to give the experts this one: *Using old strategies to face new problems can be deadly.* As Old Skugg used to say, "If the only tool you use is your teeth, every problem will look like a nut." *

* Some humans catch on faster than others. My editor tells me that a famous human behavioral theorist, Abraham Maslow, is responsible for a similar phrase. Well done, Abe!

9

Stay the course?

"To climb a tree just because it is in your path is folly."

—Old Skugg

This one is a double-edged sword. If you are making progress toward a goal, you are probably doing the right thing, assuming your goal is worthwhile and attainable. But never stop reviewing your goal, your plan to get there, and your environment. If a problem appears, e.g., a car, you must pick one, and only one, action from Column A and one, and only one, from Column B.

<u>A</u>   **<u>B</u>**

STOP   **SLOWLY**
RETREAT   **QUICKLY**
CONTINUE
CHANGE COURSE

10

A car changes all plans

"Once, when I was a young lieutenant, I led my heavily laden troops down a long-used path, only to see them cut to ribbons by enemy cross-fire. I had no plan other than scatter and run, and it cost us dearly."

—Old Skugg

Follow your plan, but don't be blind to a changing environment. You will encounter competitors along the road, and competitors like nothing more than a plodding opponent, stuck in its ways. *Always have a Plan B, and be ready to use it.* Don't be caught skittering to and fro.

11

Balance planning with action

"A battle is first lost on paper."

—Old Skugg

Some squirrels I know have never crossed the road. Oh, they plan to; in fact, they plan all the time, at the expense of action. If you spend too much time planning, whether it's strategy or tactics or budget, you are wasting valuable opportunities to act. A "perfect" plan often yields imperfect results.

Old Skugg used the following formula: "One time plan, ten times act." I think the formula changes, depending on the situation, but I think Old Skugg was on the right track.

My advice? Balance planning and action, and always remember that:
1. Balance does not mean 50 percent of this and 50 percent of that. Balance is attained when the maximum result is achieved.
2. Balance is fleeting, requiring constant adjustment to attain the maximum result.

Most important: *It's about the nuts, not the plan.*

12

Be a risk taker

"Had he but acted, the battle would have been won, but all was lost for safety's sake, and oh, how the blood did run."

—Old Skugg

With so many dead squirrels in the road, you have to wonder why we are so willing to risk it all. Let's go back to the first secret of crossing the road, *know why you are crossing the road*. Yes, it's about the nuts, stupid. A squirrel's survival depends on getting those nuts, and we know there are risks. We also know that some risks can't be avoided, that a cold winter awaits those who don't take the necessary risks to cross the road, to gather the nuts.

Every business, every organization, every army knows the "nuts" they are seeking. Every *successful* business, every *successful* organization, every *successful* army— every *successful* leader—takes calculated risks to attain those goals.

Leadership is not about playing it safe. *Be bold.*

13

Never be afraid to reverse a bad decision

"Every bad decision becomes worse when you look away."

—Old Skugg

I've made more than my share of bad decisions. Lugging acorns to my nest complete with caps was one of them. What a mess! Now I strip the caps off before tucking them into my cheeks. I can take more nuts in one trip, saving me energy. I like that.

Leaders recognize and admit bad decisions, and do their best to reverse them. They make bad decisions every day, but they are never blind to them. Enough said?

14

Be persistent—to a point

"A squirrel may climb to the top of a tree, but no higher."

—Old Skugg

If you've watched us carefully, you know that even if we've just escaped death by a hair, we will try again and again to cross the road. *A leader must be persistent in action, striving to reach a goal until it is proven unattainable.* Note, however, the distinction between persistence and stubbornness. Persistence implies firm resolve; stubbornness, being perversely unyielding. Be squirrel-headed, not bullheaded.

Part Three

20 Secrets from the Nutground

Nuts!
You must remember
Nuts!
In sweet September
Nuts!
In all their splendor
Nuts!
You must surrender!

       —Old Skugg

We are not single-minded in our pursuit of nuts—we'll eat seeds, flower buds, fruit, crops, even the occasional bird's egg or frog—but the nutground is where we work each day, and it offers up more than nuts. Here, then, are 20 leadership secrets you may find useful, or not.

15

Bury many nuts, harvest few

"Never commit your entire force at the beginning of a battle."

—Old Skugg

We squirrels bury a lot of nuts and acorns, putting them in safe keeping for another day, when hunger or the approach of winter brings us back to them. Yes, I know you will scoff at this, but thanks to our keen sense of smell, we actually do find more nuts than we lose. And we do much prefer a ground-cured nut— they are so soft and succulent—so we are persistent in our search. (We all search harder for what we think are treasures.)

But I digress. The point here is that *leaders always have more in reserve than they can use on any given day.* Whether it's cash reserves, new products in development, or additional projects or product lines, leaders always have many irons in the fire and nuts in the ground.

16

Surround yourself with ideas

"We cracked a lot of nuts, and as many jokes, but by morning, we had five good ideas for varying our attack."

—Old Skugg

Every nut, every acorn is different in some way. Which will taste best? Which will provide the fat content needed to see you through the winter? Which should be buried? Which quickly eaten or cast aside? Which is the right one for today?

The answer is, it depends. But sticking with any single acorn is as bad as having just one idea. *Leaders surround themselves with ideas and idea people, and encourage the free flow of ideas.*

17

Not all ideas bear fruit—or nuts

"They knew it was safe for them to come to me with ideas—even bad ones."

—Old Skugg

Some nuts are never as good as we hope, even after curing in the ground. So too with ideas. Don't expect every idea to be a gem. And don't expect every gem of an idea to be flawless.

Your job as leader is to encourage ideas, sort them, keep the best, fix the flawed, and reject the rest (without discouraging the flow of ideas). And remember that even good ideas have bad days.

18

Invest today for payback tomorrow

"The victory was won the day before the battle, when we stopped to sharpen our swords."

—Old Skugg

Sometimes we squirrels leave nuts in the ground by accident—we simply can't find them. Other times we intentionally leave nuts in the ground, relinquishing one nut today for a seedling that will become a sapling that will become a mature tree, providing us with shelter and sustenance in the years ahead.

Leaders do the same thing, investing in infrastructure or new ventures that show promise for helping out in the months or years ahead. *Leaders relinquish short-term gains for long-term success.*

19

Plan ahead, but not too far ahead

"Never wander into a battle."

—Old Skugg

Some humans think we are foolish to bury so many nuts; others admire us for planning ahead, for assuring that food will be there when we need it. The truth is, we do not plan as far ahead as you do. No squirrel has a five-year plan or even a two-year plan. Our goal is to get through this day and the next, and lay in a supply of nuts for the winter. Our long-term *vision* is to survive, and we have a one-year plan to get there. Focus on your vision and have a short-range, flexible plan to get there.

Long-range vision. Short-range plan.

20

Every winter is a harsh winter

"The reserve guard always grumbles till the trumpet sounds."

—Old Skugg

When we dig for nuts, we are optimists, thinking that we will find every one. But we are pessimists when we bury them, knowing that however good the supply of nuts is now, more may be needed when the snow begins to fly. A leader must balance optimism and pessimism every day, and be wise enough to know when that balance has tipped one way or the other. Fools live and die at either extreme. Leaders flourish, not in the middle, at the tipping point, but at both extremes simultaneously.

Have a bold plan, but always have a Plan B.

21

Adapt

"Nuts always appear closer in the fog."

—Old Skugg

For squirrels, every day is different. The weather changes, the soil is harder or softer, predators are there or not, and the nuts vary in location, size, and abundance. Never think you will ever reach a point where everything is predictable. Don't even think that is desirable.

Leaders readily adapt to changing conditions.

22

Be prepared to deal with a lot of nuts

"He said we should harvest the acorn caps as well, and sell them as shot glasses."

—Old Skugg

Some days I have to deal with a lot of nuts; other days, more than you can possibly imagine, whether they're nuts or nutty squirrels. As a leader, you will have to deal with both situations.

What do you do, for example, when everything goes right and you succeed beyond your wildest dreams? Some leaders and some businesses fail at this point, not knowing the dangers and pitfalls of unexpected abundance or superabundance. They are unable to cope with the new set of challenges that success brings. *You have a Plan B for the times when things go wrong; you should also have a Plan A^2 for the times when things go very right.* See also Secret 33.

Be prepared to deal with nutcases, too, those well-meaning but terribly deranged squirrels who will seek favors, offer "can't-miss" opportunities, and generally waste as much of your time as you allow.

23

There are never enough nuts

"Through good or ill, keep going. There is still much to do."

—Old Skugg

Squirrels are never satisfied with the number of nuts available to eat or bury. Neither should a leader be satisfied with the status quo, even if the status quo is untold abundance and success. *Whenever you're feeling happy about results, victories, or progress, a little voice should always whisper, "more."*

Leaders listen to the voice.

24

Select the right nuts

"Given a choice, I will attack where I can be most successful, but I will not shy away from a desperate charge if that is my only option."

—Old Skugg

We squirrels are judicious in selecting nuts. Given our druthers, we will always choose an acorn from a red oak over one from a white or a black oak, and we will always choose a large nut over a small nut. Otherwise, our energy needs would not be met and we would grow weak, sicken, and die.

As leaders, you will be faced with many decisions about "nuts." *Always opt for high-margin nuts over low-margin nuts, unless (1) only low-margin nuts are available or (2) the low-margin nut will keep you going.* See also, Secret 26.

25

Never count nuts while you gather them

"A soldier rushed up to me, a wild look in his eyes. *How many dead?* he cried. One more, and soon, I said, lest you turn and face the fight."

—Old Skugg

Leadership is about action, not about tallying. Squirrels don't stop in the middle of nut-gathering to do a nut count. Generals don't stop in the middle of a battle to count the dead and wounded. All these numbers are important, of course, but they should never interfere with the action. Have a feel for them, so you can act correctly, but don't get buried in the details until you are safely back in the nest.

Do now, count later.

26

Beware the nut-counters

"So this nut-counter strides boldly into my battle nest and directs me and my senior staff to move against the enemy. We did so without delay, tossing him straight out of the nest—to the mysteries of the night and the certainties of gravity."

—Old Skugg

It's easy to blame the nut-counters for your problems. After all, they are usually the ones who find them, at least the ones involving numbers. But don't kill the messengers; they are there to help you. On the other hand, take Old Skugg's words to heart. Never let a nut-counter do more than count nuts, report the results, and make recommendations.

Nut-counters, bless 'em, live in a world of numbers and percentages. Numbers speak to them in the night; percentages enthrall them. Accept the numbers for what they are, but reserve judgment—your judgment—on what they mean or portend. Follow these rules:

1. *Given a choice between numbers and percentages, demand both.*
2. *Never make a decision based solely on numbers or solely on percentages.*
3. *Numbers may count, but percentages don't pay the bills.*

27

Unity of purpose, not unity of thought

"Remember that old saying, *Soldier without his say, army in disarray.*"

—Old Skugg

As you can well imagine, we talk a lot about nuts and how best to gather them. What we've found is that what works best one day, doesn't the next, and that what works well for one squirrel, doesn't for another. Most important, we've found that if a squirrel has the freedom to think and to share his thoughts with the group, we all benefit.

Leadership is not a my-way-or-the-highway proposition. To demand unity of thought is to forgo unity of purpose. And without unity of purpose, you may never achieve your goals.

28

Let everyone wander around

"The consultant recommended that I limit decision-making authority in order to maintain more effective control. I told him his theory would certainly work—and be terribly wrong."

—Old Skugg

Look at the squirrels on the ground. Which one is the leader? Which the follower? You can't really tell, can you?

So too with leadership. If you are doing it right, the people you lead appear to be leaders themselves. Why? Because they are. You have given them the freedom to "wander around," literally and figuratively, to be leaders themselves. And you have not only given them responsibility for their actions, but the authority to act.

My editor tells me what I am suggesting here is called a "hands off" leadership style. I would not use that term because there is much more to it than that—and I don't really have hands. However, I do have to say that the alternative, a hands-on style, begs the question: If you have your hands on the reins all day, what are your hands free to do? Nothing but control others, limiting both you and them.

Leadership is not about control. It is about action and results. Let your people wander, let them lead. *Hands on when there's a problem, hands off otherwise.*

Letting them wander also means casting off the conventions of the past. Seat time, inflexible hours, restrictions on access to "non-work-related" information, are anachronisms. Discard them.

If leaders don't trust their staff, their staff won't trust them. *Not trusting unfrocks you as a leader, making you the obstacle to success.*

29

Never be a leader in all things

"They said I couldn't find a nut if it fell on my head, and they were right."

—Old Skugg

Even squirrels tend to lionize their leaders. Smart squirrels realize they are not lions, that they are but talented squirrels, capable of great things, yes, but not in every situation. Take Old Skugg. He was a brilliant military leader, but he had the good sense to let others lead the effort to gather nuts.

Be wise enough to know that you cannot be a leader in all things. *Lead in areas you know; let others lead in areas you don't know.* If you are good at vision but weak in day-to-day operations, find someone else to lead in that area. To attempt both is to fail in both.

30

Never be a leader at all times

"When we reached the bend in the river, I gave Colonel Sa-Lo-Li the lead so I could fall back in the ranks, commiserate with the others, share a smoke, and think about the next morning's battle."

—Old Skugg

There are squirrels I know who think they must lead all day, every day, that to relinquish "power" is a sign of weakness. To be a leader, you must show your faith in those you lead. Letting others lead is just such a show of faith, and is a sure sign of strength, not weakness.

Give others opportunities to lead, not just when you're on vacation or out of town, but when you're there to observe—and coach if need be.

31

Never eschew lesser tasks

"I could see in their smiles and thankful nods when we stopped that they knew that I knew what it was to carry a heavy pack."

—Old Skugg

I have grown quite fond of your human word *eschew*. I can almost taste the bad-nut bitterness the word evokes and see how my mouth would contort and screw up in displeasure.

Don't get caught with your face screwed up when a lesser task must be done. *Being a leader does not mean being* above *a situation, but being* in *a situation*. If nuts need to be picked up and buried, don't just stand around looking for another squirrel to do the job. Pitch in. You will gain the respect of your people and a deeper understanding of their tasks.

32

Never fear failure

"Fear hovered over the battlefield like a vulture, circling the swirling action, looking for those who could not, or would not, move."

—Old Skugg

When we work on the nutground, we expose ourselves to all manner of predators: cats, dogs, foxes, owls, hawks, weasels, the list goes on and on, and ends with humans, whose cars and traps take quite a toll. I've known squirrels so concerned about this that they spent as little time as possible collecting nuts. They are no longer chattering with us.

When you fear failure, you don't take the risks that lead to success. Yes, you will fail from time to time, perhaps fail miserably. But it is far better to fail than to never act at all.

Your job as leader is not only to act without fear, but to encourage others not to fear failure.

33

Never fear success

"A lieutenant pointed out that a victory would burden us with the care and feeding of hundreds of prisoners, and urged me to reconsider my plan. I told him I'd rather face 100 prisoners with spoons than the same hundred with swords."

—Old Skugg

I once knew a squirrel named Iplo who refused to gather the nuts we had discovered under a giant red oak. "There are too many nuts here," he said, "If I harvest them, I will have to build a bigger nest." He scampered off, leaving me scratching my head in wonder.

Success usually comes with unexpected challenges, but a leader is ready for these challenges. *You should always know what to do if you fail, and what to do if you succeed, and fear neither.*

Success is just another form of change. Embrace it, for it is a rare commodity.

34

Never seek excellence in all things

"He was bilious and unkempt, and always late, but no enemy could stand against his sword."

—Old Skugg

No squirrel is excellent in every way. We are each flawed in many, many ways. Why then should we ask each squirrel to be excellent in everything they do? We don't. We only ask that they give us their best effort in what they can do well. Our goal is to be excellent at harvesting nuts. Some of us are excellent at finding nuts, some at burying them, some at stuffing them into our cheeks, some at carrying them to our nest. But not a single one of us is excellent in every way.

A leader praises excellence, while ignoring all but the most egregious faults. And a leader never expects every facet of his operations to be excellent, but focuses instead on the one thing that is most important. *Seeking excellence in all things, whether from people or from business operations, is a fool's game.*

Part Four

10 Secrets at the Birdfeeder

"I don't know which sight is more thrilling: an army arrayed against me or a birdfeeder hung temptingly from a tree."

—Old Skugg

A birdfeeder is the most wonderful and curious contraption man ever invented. It at once shows a love for nature and a disdain for nature, feeding birds while trying (in vain) to prevent squirrels from feeding, too. But on the whole, I must thank you for even the most "squirrel-proof" feeders; that seed has helped me get through more than a few harsh winters.

The feeders, and how we defeat them, also offer up at least ten leadership secrets.

35

Never attack a competitor's strength

"They had taken great pains to guard against the obvious, an attack on their flanks, so we feigned attack there and struck dead center, where they were as soft and yielding as a flower bud."

—Old Skugg

One of the more curious things about birdfeeders is that they attempt to defeat us by attacking one of our strengths: agility. We can dangle from our hind feet and contort our bodies to defeat most feeders, eating the seed directly from the feeder or shaking it to the ground, where we and our ground-feeding bird friends can feast away.

Never attack a competitor's strength unless you are even stronger. *Every competitor has one or more weaknesses that can be readily exploited.* Find them and attack.

36

Be wary of traps

"The food was there for the taking, but because we could not reach it without exposing our entire force, we passed by, keeping to the trees, while the heady smell of it came to us on a temptress breeze."

—Old Skugg

I've seen my share of traps, especially around birdfeeders, but like any good squirrel, whenever I see easy pickings, especially food there for the taking, I keep a close eye out for traps.

Leaders must do the same. Sometimes traps present themselves as opportunities or easy advantage. I think you have an expression about free lunches that applies here, but the phrasing escapes me. *Be cautious in the face of temptation.*

37

Know your strengths—
and weaknesses

"The enemy taunted us to attack on the ground, but we were too vulnerable there, and pursued them through the trees."

—Old Skugg

A birdfeeder makes us assess our abilities, forcing us to select strength over weakness in our pursuit of food. If the feeder has a metal or plastic hood, I must realize that the footing there will be about as good as a snow covered limb, and rather than risk a fall, use other techniques to get at the seed.

Leaders are keenly aware of their strengths and weaknesses, and refuse to overestimate or underestimate either. *If you don't know your strengths and weaknesses, and honestly assess them, you can be sure your competitors do.*

38

Compete!

"You will never win a sword fight by simply parrying your opponent's blows. Thrust and thrust again, till their hearts are in their throats and their blood's upon the ground!"

—Old Skugg

I love birds as much as you do. If it weren't for them, there would be no birdfeeders, no seed. But having said that, they are also competitors who, if they had their way, would not yield up so much as a single seed to me.

Life, like it or not, is a competition. And you must lead that fight. *Compete with all your heart and all your abilities.*

39

Be opportunistic

"Every battle is won by recognizing, and taking
advantage of, decisive opportunities."

—Old Skugg

Seed in a feeder, seed on the ground, any food
anywhere, is an opportunity for a squirrel. And though
we are cautious in our approach to such opportunities,
we are persistent in our pursuit and quick to take
advantage.

*Leaders seize opportunities, even if risk and extra work will
be involved to take advantage of them.* Never leave seed
on the ground, or money on the table, if there's a safe
way to get it. And remember that if you don't take
advantage of an opportunity, someone else surely will.

40

Take advantage of competitor inefficiencies

"We hid among the corn as the farmers fired their guns, then ran again as they stopped and cursed and fumbled to reload."

—Old Skugg

Another reason we love birds is that, as beautiful as they are in flight, they are among the sloppiest and inefficient eaters on Earth, spilling seed everywhere as they cling to the feeder and peck away. I guess that's what happens when you trade hands for wings. *Every apparent advantage comes with a new weakness.*

Know your competitors as well as you know yourself,

and take advantage of their every weakness and

inefficiency.

41

Be wary of competitors

"We paid too much attention to the skirmish at hand and not to the force marching against us from behind."

—Old Skugg

Birdfeeders bring out the worst and best of everyone involved. We bring our skills to the table to take advantage of the hospitality you show the birds. The birds bring their inefficiencies. You bring your "squirrel-proof" devices and traps. And both we and the birds attract predators with their own food plans.

Be wary of competitors—not just the ones that compete directly in your market, but the ones that seek to gobble you up.

42

Avoid distractions

"We fell upon them when they were tired, and distracted by the rain."

—Old Skugg

Birdseed is an opportunity we readily pursue, but we never let it distract us to the point that we are consumed by competitors or forget that our main business is not seed but nuts.

Don't let an opportunity distract you from your core activity. *Take advantage of an opportunity; don't let it take advantage of you.*

43

Be wary of easy pickings

"Be careful of putting two words together: *easy* and *victory*."

—Old Skugg

Birdseed on the ground is about as easy as it gets for a squirrel. But fast food comes with its perils. I've lost more than a few friends who speedily and greedily consumed seed before giving it so much as a sniff to detect poison.

Things that come easily must be examined as intensely as things that come hard.

44

Innovate!

"If you want to see confusion, attack your enemy in a novel, unexpected way."

—Old Skugg

If you have ever watched a squirrel or team of squirrels attack a birdfeeder, particularly a "squirrel-proof" birdfeeder, you have probably seen them do amazing things. Don't get a birdfeeder to watch birds, get one to watch squirrels!

You will see us bouncing on tree limbs to shake seed from the feeder. You will see us hop quickly to and off the feeder to get it swinging like a pendulum to make it drop seed to the ground with every swing. You will see us hanging upside down from a twig to reach the feeder. You will see us gnawing through wooden posts to bring the feeder down. You will see us fall, time and again, without the slightest fear. You will see— innovation!

Leaders innovate to gain advantage. And they encourage and reward innovation, top to bottom, in their organizations.

Part Five

4 Secrets from a Squirrel's Tail

"The army swept across the field in gray waves, devastating everything in its path."

—Old Skugg

Admit it, you are fascinated by the tail of a squirrel. So puffy in repose. So graceful in action, making us look like little waves rippling across your lawn.

But the tail of a squirrel has much to teach, too. Here, then, are four leadership secrets to keep or swish aside.

45

You're not in this alone

"We moved as one, like some fierce, multi-headed beast, the enemy awe-struck, scattering before us, unable to withstand our charge."

—Old Skugg

My tail is a daily reminder that what follows me, balances me. Wherever I jump, the tail follows—to a point. If I make a mistake, say, by misjudging the distance between one branch and another, the tail always knows, and does its best to adjust my momentum to assure a safe landing.

Leaders know they do not, cannot, act alone, that the tail is as important as the head. Whether you're a CEO or a supervisor, a general or a squad leader, leadership is not about having people work for you, but *with* you.

Rank may have its privileges, but leadership is not one of them.

46

Maintain balance

"The foolish charge in the driving rain, the wide-eyed pause as the lightning struck, tore our balanced charge asunder, forcing a retreat through mud and blood and distant thunder."

—Old Skugg

The tail is also a reminder that you must have balance in everything you do. To be overly aggressive or aggressively meek is to invite disaster. My tail provides the balance between what is possible and what is unlikely, and helps me attain in two leaps what I first thought could be attained in one.

Do not confuse balance with conservatism, however. *Balance is not about being conservative, but being precise in a fluid, ever-changing environment.*

And, as I pointed out in Secret 11, remember that balance is rarely a 50-50 proposition. Each leap may require a different balance of actions to maximize results.

47
Watch your back

"They called her Colonel Tail-Eye, so uncanny were her abilities to detect and rebuff surprise attacks."

—Old Skugg

Ever see a squirrel with a bent tail, or a partial tail, or no tail at all? That's because we do our best to avoid the no-squirrel-at-all scenario. When we sense danger, we curl our tail up over our back to make sure that, if an enemy does attack, we give up a tail rather than our life.

Never get so caught up in what you're doing that you become unaware of competitors sneaking up behind you.

48

Appear larger than life

"My voice boomed, my tail thrashed, the very tree seemed to shake as I drove them into battle. When they left, I looked in the mirror, waggled my eyebrows, and called myself a puffed up old scalawag."

—Old Skugg

Arching our tails over our backs also makes us look bigger than we actually are, creating doubt in the minds of competitors and awe in the minds of our followers. Both creations of mind can be used to good purpose. Appearing larger than life is an act that we have mastered.

You can master this, too. But always remember two things:

1. *The technique should be used only when needed, not every day, and*
2. *You are not really larger than life—ever.* (You are just acting.)

So, like any good actor, hit the mark, say the words, take the nuts.

Part Six

10 Secrets in the Trees

"Oh, to be in the treeways of my full-sapped youth, to sway in the branches, and 'round the tree trunks run."

—Old Skugg

Where would squirrels be without trees? They provide us with food, shelter, and safety and ask nothing in return save dispersal of their nuts and acorns. And even that in a soft whisper.

Trees and how we use them also offer up ten leadership secrets.

49

See the forest—and the trees

"In a mighty oak, on a branch above the drey, I found my obsylarium and dreamed throughout the day."

—Old Skugg

The branches directly above a nest, or drey as we call it, are known as an obsylarium. Actually, the squirrel word is unpronounceable by humans, so I've taken three familiar human words—observation, sylvan, and solarium—to translate the essence of the squirrel word. An obsylarium is a place for deep reflection and objective observation, where you can see both forest and trees, feel the heat of the sun, sway with the tree, and listen to the secrets whispered by the wind.

I am not suggesting that you climb a tree, unless of course, you never did so as a child. What I am suggesting is this: *Leaders take the time to step back and review what they're doing, see the big picture, and make necessary adjustments*. See also, Secret 5.

50

Always put a tree between yourself and danger

"How many times have I thanked this tree for assuring my invisibility."

—Old Skugg

How many times have you seen a squirrel scramble out of sight behind a tree trunk to avoid you? Probably a lot. We do this because it works—and because it's great fun to see dogs barking up the wrong tree! Predators can neither see us nor reach us, assuring our safety.

Leaders—even the boldest leaders—make contingencies to assure their safety. Fallback positions, reserve funds, core business areas, all are trees between you and danger. Have as many as you need, but don't spend all day behind them.

51

Have lofty but achievable goals

"Climb high, but remember that while branches may bend, twigs will break."

—Old Skugg

A squirrel's nest is typically in the top one-third of a tree, but never at the very top, where the branches offer little support and the nest would be vulnerable to predators. We seek the heights but know that going too high is dangerous.

Leaders know what lies within their grasp—and beyond it.

52

Select the right tree(s)

"We set up our base drey in a tall maple in a stand of seven trees, providing a clear view of the nutground and ample treeways for tactical and evasive maneuvers."

—Old Skugg

Any tree I select to build a nest in must meet several criteria. It must be:

- Near the nutground, so I can keep a close eye on everything
- Close enough to give me a rapid escape route in case of danger
- Tall enough to discourage the pursuit of cats, but not so tall that I expend too much energy reaching my drey
- One of a stand of closely spaced trees, providing me with multiple treeways for escape, avoidance, and evasion

Choose your base of operations carefully. *Where you act may be as important as why, when, and how you act.* My editor wants me to insert "location, location, location" here, but it seems a bit redundant.

53

Embrace change

Trees in leafy show
Arrange to change
For winter's snow.

　　　—Old Skugg

I change my nest at least twice a year. My summer drey
is really not much more than a platform of twigs and
leaves where I can sleep through the muggy nights
without fear of falling. My winter drey, as you might
suspect, is more elaborate. I construct this out of twigs
and leaves, making a waterproof home I line with moss,
bark, feathers, and scavenged cardboard for warmth.
But if I see a better opportunity, say a shed with easy
access, I'll abandon my drey for the shed's added
warmth and security.

I am proud of my dreys, but not so proud that I stay in
them when conditions change and advantage might be
lost by remaining.

*Leaders are sensitive to changing conditions and readily
embrace change, even when it means giving up "nests" that
have served them well.*

Change.

54

Be flexible in all things

"I could see General Katerica, his nose pressed to his battle plan, sending wave after wave to their deaths, and my heart sank."

—Old Skugg

Ever climb a tree when the wind made it sway, when it refused to be rigid against a force it could not stay? Ever notice how the taller trees sway more than the smaller ones? Ah, the wisdom of trees, to know that all organizations require flexibility and each in direct proportion to its size.

Leaders remain flexible in all things, building flexibility into their plans, their organizations, and how they and their staff approach each day.

55

Integrate work and play

"The solution came to me as I gamboled with my family on the treeways of an oak."

—Old Skugg

Everything I do is about what I do. When I am home in my tree, I think about home—and work. When I'm at work on the nutground, I think about work—and home. My survival depends on it.

And so does yours. Ignore the advice to segregate your life at work from your life at home. There is only one life. *To live life fully, and wisely, you must bring work to your home and home, and play, to your work.*

Leaders integrate work and play, for themselves and their staff.

56

Seek and take advice

"No sooner were the words out of my mouth when I realized the faults in my plan and saw them mirrored in the knowing nod of my thirty-second wife."

—Old Skugg

Although some of us live solitary lives in our dreys, most (including me) prefer the company of family and friends. It would not be unheard of, for example, to have as many as a dozen squirrels living in the same drey. We take advantage of our dreymates by seeking their advice and counsel on matters large and small. It is in the drey where we learn our first important lessons, for example, *never put your tongue on a frozen acorn.*

Seek advice from family, friends, and colleagues, and take it if it makes sense to you. *Sometimes just seeking advice and framing a problem for others will lead you to a solution.*

57

Retreat and replenish

"Not being there is sometimes the only way to truly be there."

—Old Skugg

Even though we integrate work and play every single day, squirrels still need a break every now and then to retreat from the everyday and replenish our spirits—and our focus.

Take a step back, at home and at work, by taking a vacation or holding a work retreat. You'll be surprised at how quickly the trees become a forest again, and how much the forest has changed in your absence.

58

Avoid dogs—and dogma

"Round and round the tree trunk run, chasing consultants one by one."

—Old Skugg

Why do dogs hate us so? I cannot fathom it, but I am never far from my tree when dogs are around. I don't want to end up like poor Mungo, the poor squirrel whose epitaph appears at the front of this book and who was ripped apart by a shepherd dog—even if some Benjamin Franklin were around to memorialize the event in words.

You face "dogs" every day, so you will need a safe place where you can avoid their fangs or, in the case of consultants, their dogma. Ever notice squirrels chasing each other around a tree trunk? Well, one of those squirrels is usually a consultant. (The trick is knowing who's chasing whom.) For more on them, turn the page.

Part Seven

4 Secrets about Owls

"Accept an owl's wisdom, but beware its beak and talons."

—Old Skugg

It's fitting that we end this little book with a discussion of consultants because it loops us back to where we began and bookends a troublesome topic, *Leadership Theory*, the cash acorn of many consultants.

In *The Obsylarium*, Old Skugg sets forth definitions for experts and consultants:

Expert—*Someone who knows his stuff, but not yours.*

Consultant—*An expert you pay to tell you what you already know, much to the chagrin of your staff, who usually know better.*

I'm not sure I agree completely with Old Skugg, but the old boy does make his points. At Consolidated Acorns, Inc., I deal with a lot of consultants, and have learned at least three valuable secrets from them: accept their wisdom, reject their wisdom, and beware their beaks and talons. Oh, and there's a fourth secret, too. But more on that later.

59

Accept an owl's wisdom

"Sutwithn wanted desperately to rewrite the battle plan, but I only needed his recommendations on the placement and array of the catapults."

—Old Skugg

Squirrels don't much like owls; they're a blood-thirsty lot, especially during a full moon. Old Skugg knew this, but still used an owl named Sutwithn, on occasion, to assess problems involving aerial distances and trajectories. I won't get into the technicalities of that. Suffice to say that, since you humans use owls to symbolize wisdom, I will, too.

Some consultants are wise owls, with much to teach; others are wise in their ways and merely seek to insinuate themselves into everything you do, for their own gain.

Leaders know the difference and only hire consultants in areas where they *and their staff* agree that they lack the wisdom, skills, or experience to proceed. *In most cases, you should hire a consultant to recommend, not to do.*

60

Reject an owl's wisdom

"The problem, according to Sutwithn, was that we were in the wrong business, that nut-gathering was a low-margin business with a dismal Return on Investment, or ARE-HOOOO-EYE, as he called it."

—Old Skugg

The good consultants' evil twins will analyze your business, tell you what you're doing wrong, and help you unleash the corrective carnage required to implement *their vision*.

If you want to dismantle your company, lower profits, lose competitive advantage, become less efficient, and lower morale, the twins are waiting in the wings, as eager as snake-oil salesmen or evangelists to begin their work and settle in for the long haul.

Hire consultants only to do very targeted projects of brief, pre-defined duration. *Never let a consultant's vision replace yours.*

Beware an owl's beak and talons

"I had only to mention the wealth of my enemy to Sutwithn, and he was off like a shot, flapping gleefully toward their lines. Oh, that was a happy day."

—Old Skugg

The beak of an owl is made for ripping and tearing flesh; its talons, for holding, grasping, and inflicting pain and submission. If an owl tells you he's doing this to you for your own good, you may have the wrong owl.

Beware the consultant's beak and talons:

- Open-ended projects
- Organization-wide, in-depth analyses
- Retainers
- Hourly rates
- Exclusive agreements

And remember that their plans often *appear* to be worthwhile:

- New visions
- New leadership theories

- Strategic reorganization
- Improved efficiencies
- Improved bottom-lir 79

Hire an owl, if you must, but be cautious.

62

Avoid the rubber acorn

"The last thing I need is another speaking engagement at a rubber acorn dinner."

—Old Skugg

In Secret 58, I warned you about the dogma of consultants. Now I must warn you about *squirrelma*. Anyone who writes a book on leadership is *ipso facto* a consultant. So I guess, in a way, I am a consultant, too. My fee was the price of this book.

When you buy a book on leadership (or any topic where you're seeking advice or understanding), think of the book as a thick business card for the authors, many of whom write books in order to get speaking engagements and consulting work.

Fortunately, since I'm a squirrel, I have no plans for either, at least in your world. And besides, I don't think it would be in your best interest to hire a squirrel as a consultant, if you know what I mean. Perception is everything, so not many people would understand.

Likewise, I don't want you to adopt each and every secret in this book. Remember, it's a collection of tools, nothing more. *Use the ones that work for you, or none at all.*

Last Leaf

"I could be wrong, I suppose."

—Old Skugg

Those were Old Skugg's last words, spoken as he lay upon his leafy bed in the High Drey, surrounded by family and friends, just days after completing *The Obsylarium*. Two centuries later, *The Obsylarium* still speaks to squirrels. I hope the excerpts I selected spoke to you as well, and that you've squirrel-eared a few pages for future reference. The choices are yours, after all.

Leadership, in the final analysis, is about *making choices*—the right choices—when it counts, and dealing effectively with the bad choices along the way. Easy to say, hard to do.

Leadership is also about *letting go* and *moving on*. It is time for me to do both, to get back to my day job at Consolidated Acorns, Inc. And it is time for you to go back to Part One and dig up the theory you buried there for safe keeping—if you can find it. I wonder, has it changed?

I wish I had time to accompany you there, but I have nuts of my own to find. So many nuts, so little time.

Be the squirrel.

—SIMON SILVERBACK

Appendix A

Translator's Notes

Translation of leaftext in Sciuriniskrit is a daunting task, made more difficult by the rapid deterioration of the leaves used as the text medium. Unlike Chitterlian, the spoken language of the Sciurinae—the subfamily of squirrels to which Simon Silverback and Lindar the Elder belong—Sciuriniskrit is both ephemeral and multidimensional. (The leaftext for the book you have just read, in fact, is essentially unreadable now.)

The challenge for the translator is to quickly decipher the markings made by claw and tooth before the ravages of temperature and humidity distort or obscure meaning. Fortunately, the writing and translating took place simultaneously, with Simon at my side to correct and guide me through the nuances— and there are many!—of his written language.

Consider the challenges. First, the same passage written on an oak leaf has an altogether *different* meaning from the same passage on a maple leaf, the oak reserved for serious discourse, the maple for satire. In all, seven different varieties of leaves were used in the leaftext, each providing a nuance.

Second, the scratch marks on the tops of the leaves could only be interpreted by taking into account the position and depth of bite marks on both sides of the leaf, making it truly a three-dimensional language. Here,

I had to rely on Simon's re-reading, with him taking the leaf into his mouth to gauge depth and then reporting the results in Chitterlian, a language I must say has caused me embarrassment when I inadvertently resort to it in public. (Although it is a good way to get a seat on the subway!)

Third, my own limitations as a translator slowed the process. My area of expertise is in the written language of the Pteromyinae, or flying squirrels, whose ability to scratch leaves is somewhat inhibited by the anatomy of their hands, particularly the bones, ligaments, and muscles of the wrist. The result is a much finer and altogether different script, with few nuances.

Fourth, Simon himself provided a whole set of difficulties, most notably his short attention span and a predilection for straying from the subject to quote passages from *The Obsylarium*.

Finally, *The Obsylarium* itself, which was written in Old Sciuriniskrit in the 18th Century and dutifully transcribed over and over by the Marmotini Monks, had lost through iteration any semblance of the original. Much of it, sadly, had to be discarded. Fortunately, though, the Sciurinae have a strong oral tradition, so Simon was able to fill in the blanks in most cases.

The result, I hope, is clear, intelligible, and worthwhile.

—LEN BOSWELL

Appendix B

Famous Humans on Squirrels

Over the centuries, a few notable humans have found us of special interest and have incorporated us into their works as exemplars of beauty, nature, industry, grace, and wildness, among other things . . .

I know that something akin to the migratory instinct in birds . . . is known to have affected the squirrel tribe, impelling them to a general and mysterious movement, in which they were seen, say some, crossing the broadest rivers, each on its particular chip, with its tail raised for a sail, and bridging narrower streams with their dead.
> —Henry David Thoreau, *Walking*

O sweet September, thy first breezes bring
The dry leaf's rustle and the squirrel's laughter,
The cool fresh air whence health and vigor spring
And promise of exceeding joy hereafter.
> —George Arnold, *September Days*

A squirrel leaping from bough to bough, and making the wood but one wide tree for his pleasure, fills the eye

not less than a lion—is beautiful, self-sufficing, and
stands then and there for nature.
                    —Ralph Waldo Emerson, *Essays*

A headless squirrel, some blood
oozing from the unevenly
chewed-off neck
lies in rainsweet grass
near the woodshed door.
                    —Denise Levertov, *A Day Begins*

The squirrel hoards nuts and the bee gathers honey,
without knowing what they do, and they are thus
provided for without selfishness or disgrace.
                    —Ralph Waldo Emerson, *In the Dial*

I wondered how he could call any particular tree there
his home; and yet he would run up the stem of one out
of the myriads, as if it were an old road to him. How
can a hawk ever find him there? I fancied that he must
be glad to see us, though he did seem to chide us.
        —Henry David Thoreau, *The Maine Woods*

Come play with me;
Why should you run
Through the shaking tree
As though I'd a gun
To strike you dead?
                    —William Butler Yeats, *The Wild Swans at Coole*

If we had a keen vision and feeling of all ordinary
human life, it would be like hearing the grass grow and
the squirrel's heart beat, and we should die of that roar
which lies on the other side of silence. As it is, the best
of us walk about well wadded with stupidity.
—George Eliot, *Middlemarch*

He obeys the orders of nature
Without knowing them
It is what he does not know
That makes him beautiful.
Such a knot of little purposeful nature!
—Richard Eberhart, *On a Squirrel Crossing the
Road in Autumn*

He had ragged long grass-coloured hair;
He had knees that stuck out of his hose;
He had puddle-water in his shoes;
He had half a cloak to keep him dry,
Although he had a squirrel's eye.
—William Butler Yeats, *Baile and Aillinn*

Talents differ; all is well and wisely put;
If I cannot carry forests on my back,
Neither can you crack a nut.
—Ralph Waldo Emerson, *The Mountain and the Squirrel*

I have a venturous fairy that shall seek
The squirrel's hoard, and fetch thee thence new nuts.
—William Shakespeare, *A Midsummer-Night's Dream, Act
IV, Scene I*

Her chariot is an empty hazel-nut,
Made by the joiner squirrel or old grub,
Time out o' mind the fairies' coach-makers.
And in this state she gallops night by night
Through lovers' brains, and then they dream of love.
—William Shakespeare, *Romeo and Juliet, Act I, Scene IV*

I recollect that, when a stripling, my first exploit in
squirrel-shooting was in a grove of tall walnut-trees
that shades one side of the valley.
—Washington Irving, *The Legend of Sleepy Hollow*

With that he made off up the sliding deck like a
squirrel, and plunged into the cabin.
—Robert Louis Stevenson, *The Master of Ballantrae*

In the forest of Arden it was said that down to modern
times a squirrel might leap from tree to tree for nearly
the whole length of Warwickshire.
—Sir James George Frazer, *The Golden Bough*

On a stout old beech at the edge, decayed and slanting,
almost fallen to the stream, yet with life and leaves in
its mossy limbs, a gray squirrel, exploring, runs up and
down, flirts his tail, leaps to the ground, sits on his
haunches upright as he sees me, (a Darwinian hint?) and
then races up the tree again.
—Walt Whitman, *Specimen Days*

Being out of heart with government
I took a broken root to fling
Where the proud, wayward squirrel went,
Taking delight that he could spring;
And he, with that low whinnying sound

That is like laughter, sprang again
And so to the other tree at a bound.
Nor the tame will, nor timid brain,
Bred that fierce tooth and cleanly limb
And threw him up to laugh on the bough;
No government appointed him.
—William Butler Yeats, *Responsibilities and Other Poems*

O what can ail thee, knight-at-arms!
So haggard and so woe-begone?
The squirrel's granary is full
And the harvest's done.
　　　—John Keats, *La Belle Dame Sans Merci*

The squirrel leaps among the boughs,
And chatters in his leafy house.
　　　—John Townsend Trowbridge, *Midsummer*

Trees was all around us, a-whisperin' cheering words;
Loud was the squirrel's chatter, and sweet the songs of
birds.
　　　—Will Carleton, *Out of the Old House, Nancy*

A sweet and playful Highland girl,
As light and beauteous as a squirrel,
As beauteous and as wild!
　　　　　—William Wordsworth, *A Tale*

The wildness of squirrels is an awesome wildness.
　　　—Douglas Fairbairn, *A Squirrel of His Own*

Like a small grey coffee pot sits the squirrel.
　　—Humbert Wolfe, *The Grey Squirrel*

The steeples swam in amethyst, the news like squirrels
swam.
　　—Emily Dickinson, *I'll Tell You How the Sun Rose*

I'm dead sick of parties, and flirtations, trying to out-
dress my neighbors, and going the same round year
after year, like a squirrel in a cage.
　　—Louisa May Alcott, *An Old-fashioned Girl*

She was the child of a poor woman who lived in the
forest--a wild little thing, always dancing and singing
about; as hard to catch as a squirrel, and so fearless she
would climb the highest trees, leap broad brooks, or
jump off the steep rocks to show her courage.
　　—Louisa May Alcott, *Jack and Jill*

A squirrel in a cage who pats the nuts which it cannot
eat, as if to bury them in the ground, can hardly be
thought to act thus, either from pleasure or pain.
Hence the common assumption that men must be
impelled to every action by experiencing some pleasure
or pain may be erroneous.
　　—Charles Darwin, *Descent of Man*

A squirrel, from the lofty depths of his domestic tree,
chattered either in anger or merriment—for the
squirrel is such a choleric and humorous little
personage, that it is hard to distinguish between his
moods—so he chattered at the child, and flung down a

nut upon her head. It was a last year's nut, and already gnawed by his sharp tooth.

—Nathaniel Hawthorne, *The Scarlet Letter*

Paul is a squirrel turned into a man. He has its bright, quick eyes, its hair, its pointed nose, its small, fine, supple, active body, and a certain mysterious resemblance in his general bearing; in fact, a similarity of movement, of gesture, and of bearing which might almost be taken for a recollection.

—Guy de Maupassant, *The Rondoli Sisters*

He is an exceptional man, is that M. Colbert. He does not love you—that is very possible; but, mordioux! the squirrel can guard himself against the adder with very little trouble.

—Alexandre Dumas, *The Man in the Iron Mask*

Of all beasts he learned the language,
Learned their names and all their secrets,
How the beavers built their lodges,
Where the squirrels hid their acorns,
How the reindeer ran so swiftly,
Why the rabbit was so timid,
Talked with them whene'er he met them,
Called them "Hiawatha's Brothers."

—Henry Wadsworth Longfellow, *Hiawatha's Childhood*

A couple of squirrels set on a limb and jabbered at me very friendly.
>
> —Mark Twain, *Huckleberry Finn*

To add to the gloom, almost every living thing seems to have departed, and not a whistle of a bird nor the bark of the squirrel can be heard in this solitude.
>
> —Mark Twain, *Life on the Mississippi*

Within this shell were shut up a large cat, and a squirrel belonging to J. T. Maston, and of which he was particularly fond. They were desirous, however, of ascertaining how this little
animal, least of all others subject to giddiness, would endure this experimental voyage.
>
> —Jules Verne, *From the Earth to the Moon*

She drew a cluster of pins from her mouth, in which she seemed to secret them as squirrels stow away nuts.
>
> —Edith Wharton, *The Bunner Sisters*

In that squirrel-wheel of a world of his and Susy's you had to keep going or drop out—and Susy, it was evident, had chosen to keep going.
>
> —Edith Wharton, *The Glimpses of the Moon*

The wood birds sang merrily above his head; the squirrels, whisking their bravery of tail, ran barking from tree to tree, unconscious of the pity of it, and somewhere far away was a strange, muffed thunder, as if the partridges were drumming in celebration of

nature's victory over the son of her immemorial enslavers.
—Ambrose Bierce, *Chickamauga*

They were worried that I, an educated man with a knowledge of languages, should, instead of devoting myself to science or literary work, live in the country, rush round like a squirrel in a rage, work hard with never a penny to show for it.
—Anton Chekhov, *About Love*

He threw a pine cone at a jovial squirrel, and he ran with chattering fear. High in a treetop he stopped, and, poking his head cautiously from behind a branch, looked down with an air of trepidation.
—Stephen Crane, *The Red Badge of Courage*

Man, Watson, man. Only one, but a very formidable person. Strong as a lion—witness the blow that bent that poker! Six foot three in height, active as a squirrel, dexterous with his fingers, finally, remarkably quick-witted, for this whole ingenious story is of his concoction.
—Arthur Conan Doyle, *The Return of Sherlock Holmes*

The bijou mountains were densely wooded and were infested by ferocious squirrels and woodpeckers that forever menaced the summer transients.
—O Henry, *To Him Who Waits*

But I hate ecstasy, Dionysic or any other. It's like going round in a squirrel cage.
—D. H. Lawrence, *Women in Love*

A squirrel, running around the base of the trunk, came full upon him, and gave him a great fright. He cowered down and snarled. But the squirrel was as badly scared. It ran up the tree, and from a point of safety chattered back savagely.

—Jack London, *White Fang*

In the silence that fell, she continued her caressing of his hair, while she idly watched a great gray squirrel, boisterous and hilarious, as it scampered back and forth in a distant vista of the redwoods.

—Jack London, *Planchette*

His dress was a tunic of forest green, furred at the throat and cuffs with what was called minever; a kind of fur inferior in quality to ermine, and formed, it is believed, of the skin of the grey squirrel.

—Sir Walter Scott, *Ivanhoe*

You can't be suspicious of a tree, or accuse a bird or a squirrel of subversion or challenge the ideology of a violet.

—Hal Borland, *Sundial of the Seasons*

The squirrel that you kill in jest, dies in earnest.

—Henry David Thoreau, *Familiar Letters*

His bony hand dug its way like a squirrel into his overall pocket, brought out a black, bitten plug of tobacco.

—John Steinbach, *The Grapes of Wrath*

Why waste your final hours racing about your cage denying you're a squirrel?
> —Ray Bradbury, *Fahrenheit 451*

Over here's the bird feeder, where the squirrels terrorize the chicadees.
> —John Updike, *Seek My Face*

The copper beech by their old bedroom, with the nuts that would pop on their own all night, attracted the squirrels, she would say, making her lap and setting her hands on her knees as if God had cooked up squirrels just to bedevil her.
> —John Updike, *Rabbit at Rest*

Agitated squirrels tousle it, clambering out on its downward-drooping twigs, and then scamper thunderously across the roof above my head.
> —John Updike, *Toward the End of Time*

The first living creature I met was a partridge, which sprang up beneath my feet, and whirred away; the next was a squirrel, who chattered angrily at me from an overhanging bough.
> —Nathaniel Hawthorne, *The Blithedale Romance*

I lay down on a branch and, leaning my head against the trunk, went hastily to sleep while a squirrel of my whim sat stiff-tailed at the trembling end of a branch, and rocked itself.
> —Franz Kafka, *Description of a Struggle*

Ratatosk (in Norse myth, a squirrel whose name means "swift teeth," lives in the World Tree called Yggdrasil, and is a notorious gossip).
>—Caroline Myss, *Sacred Contracts*

His pale eyes accentuated his look of a sailor and his small moustache looked like the fur of a squirrel.
—Gabriel Garcia Marquez, *One Hundred Years of Solitude*

A squirrel moved along a limb in a flowing motion, a passage so continuous it seemed to be its own physical law, different from the ones we've learned to trust.
>—Don Delillo, *White Noise*

The squirrel popped out of the puckered mouth of its hole like a tongue, checked on the trunk, and then spied a likely-looking bit of nest fodder.
>—Stephen King, *Skeleton Crew*

She was like a squirrel, with hidden pouches for the future.
>—M.F.K. Fisher, *Long Ago in France*

And only in New York, yesterday I saw a nut gathering squirrels.
>—David Letterman, *The Late Show*

About the authors

Simon Silverback is founder and CEO of Consolidated Acorns, Inc., an international acorn-processing company. A graduate of the University of Maryland's famed High Tree/Open Window program, he has held executive positions in many for-profit and not-for-profit organizations. He now lives in a tall oak tree in Berkeley Springs, West Virginia, with his thirty-second wife.

Len Boswell, Simon's editor, translator, and confidant, is a former publishing executive who likes to think he treasured his staff more than his leadership ideas. In any event, he has now turned rogue, writing novels and such under Simon's tree. It has been said by some that on any given fall day, you can see him and Simon gamboling through the leaves.

Printed in Great Britain
by Amazon